ACTION SPORTS

FREESTYLE MOTOCROSS

By K. A. Hale

Kaleidoscope
Minneapolis, MN

The Quest for Discovery Never Ends

This edition is co-published by agreement between Kaleidoscope and World Book, Inc.

Kaleidoscope Publishing, Inc.
6012 Blue Circle Drive
Minnetonka, MN 55343 U.S.A.

World Book, Inc.
180 North LaSalle St., Suite 900
Chicago IL 60601 U.S.A.

Kaleidoscope ISBNs
978-1-64519-065-3 (library bound)
978-1-64494-146-1 (paperback)
978-1-64519-166-7 (ebook)

World Book ISBN
978-0-7166-4358-6 (library bound)

Library of Congress Control Number
2019938877

Printed in the United States of America.

Bigfoot lurks within one of the images in this book. It's up to you to find him!

TABLE OF CONTENTS

CHAPTER 1

THE X GAMES

Tom Pagès is nervous. He is a freestyle motocross (FMX) rider from France. He's competing at the 2018 X Games in Minnesota. Each rider gets two runs. Both runs are scored. Only the best score counts.

His first run didn't go well. Pagès only scored forty-four points. He messed up his first jump. He was in the wrong gear. He did a straight jump off the ramp. Straight jumps don't impress the judges.

FMX TRICKS

There are four kinds of tricks in FMX. Right-side-up tricks are done with the bike upright. In backflip variations, the rider does a trick while doing a backflip. For a body varial, the rider spins or flips their body around the bike. Flair tricks are custom tricks done off a quarterpipe.

Pagès had won most big freestyle contests. He won his first Red Bull X-Fighters competition five years ago. But he hadn't won at the X Games.

Athletes do high-flying tricks on their dirt bikes. Dirt bikes are a type of motorcycle.

Pagès knows he could get hurt if something goes wrong. Earlier, a rider dislocated his shoulder. Another rider popped it back in. One rider fell and crashed his bike. Pagès has fallen in other competitions. He had to miss the X Games last year. His shoulder was hurt.

Pagès starts his run. The track has a **roll-in** ramp. It also has ramps on the ground. There are quarterpipes, too. There are dirt landings all around. He does a double backflip. Then he does a body varial and a **360**.

Freestyle motocross tracks feature many dirt ramps and landings for athletes to use in doing tricks.

Tom Pagès's impressive FMX tricks have won him many competitions.

Now it's time for his **signature move**. It's called the bike flip. His bike is 33 pounds (15 kg) lighter than most bikes.

He needs that for this trick. He goes off a quarterpipe. He spins his bike around next to him. Then he gets back on the bike to land. The crowd loves it. He does two more tricks and lands them both. He's on fire! Then he ends with one last trick. He lets go of his bike in the air. He grasps the grab holes on his bike seat. He pulls himself back on. He lands!

The crowd goes wild. He scores a 92.33! Pagès finally wins his X Games gold medal.

FUN FACT

Each run at the X Games is seventy-five seconds.

CHAPTER 2

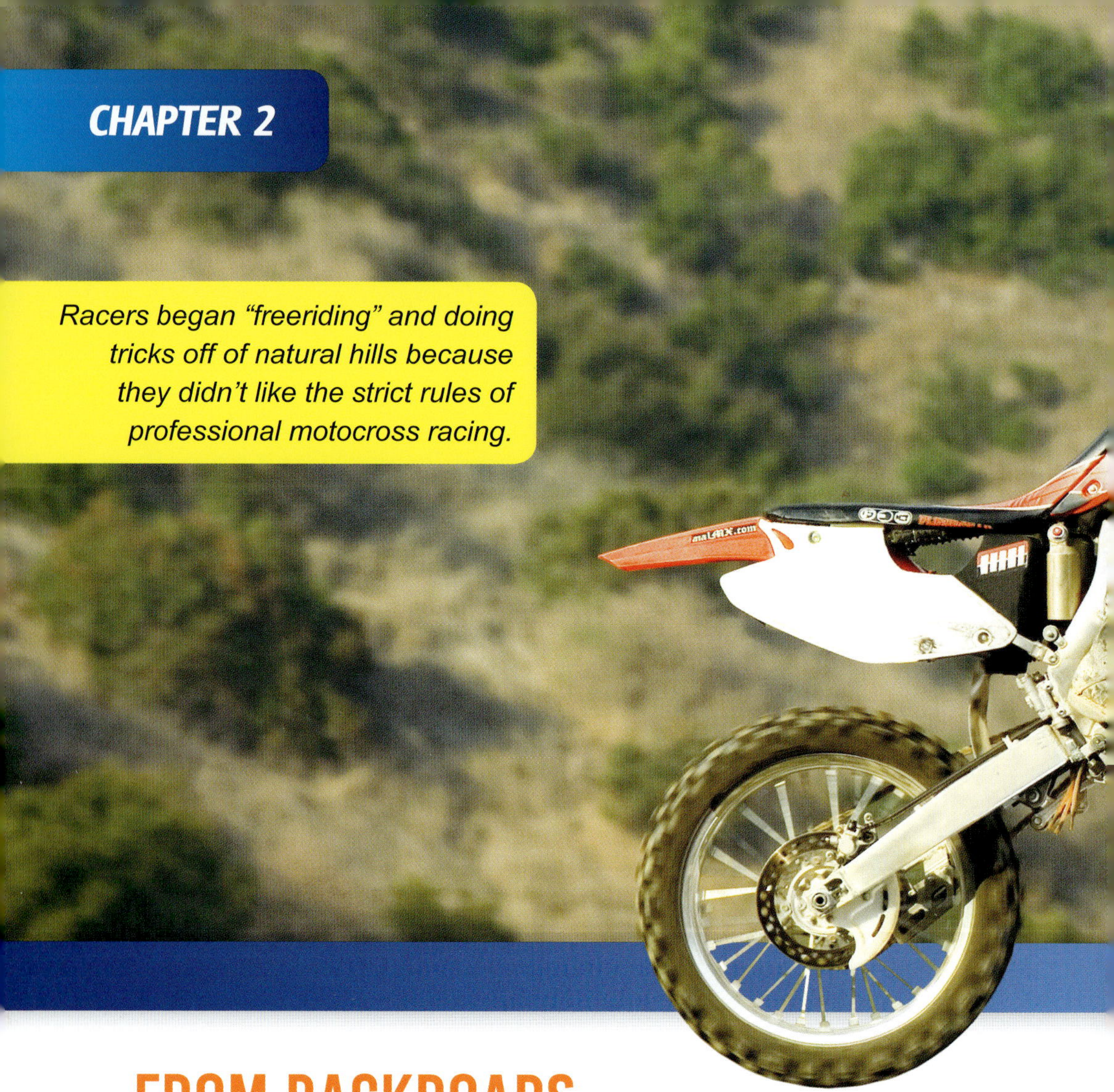

Racers began "freeriding" and doing tricks off of natural hills because they didn't like the strict rules of professional motocross racing.

FROM BACKROADS TO BULLRINGS

Competitive motorcycle racing started after World War I (1914–1918). The sport became known as motocross. Motocross came to the United States. It was the 1960s. But professional racing was tightly controlled by **sponsors**. The riders wanted more freedom. They started doing tricks off natural hills. They called this "freeriding."

One day, two filmmakers saw these riders. They thought it would be perfect for a movie. They filmed *Crusty Demons of Dirt*. This movie showed riders doing tricks. It set the clips to cool music. This movie brought FMX to the public's attention.

FMX made motorcycle companies nervous. Bikes weren't made to be used this way. They thought people might get hurt. But riders were excited. The first official FMX contest was in 1998. The contest was popular. The X Games added FMX the next year.

FUN FACT

X-fighters uses 3,600 tons (3,266 metric tons) of dirt in each event.

Red Bull started a competition in 2001. It was called Red Bull X-Fighters. The first one was in a bullring in Spain. In 2005, X-Fighters became a world tour. X-Fighters has had more than fifty shows all over the world. In 2010, they performed at the Pyramids of Giza in Egypt.

Many people come to Red Bull X-Fighters events.

FREESTYLE MOTOCROSS RECORDS

First backflip

Carey Hart (performed, 2000), Mike Metzger (landed, 2002)

First double backflip

Travis Pastrana, 2006

Longest ramp-to-ramp backflip on a motorcycle

Cameron Sinclair, 129 feet 7 inches (39.49 m), 2008

First front flip

Jim DeChamp, 2008

First front flip landed in competition

Jackson "Jacko" Strong, 2011

A new action sports competition started in 2016. It was the Nitro World Games. It came from the Nitro Circus tour. The Nitro World Games is a one-night competition. People can watch it on TV. The first double front flip was landed at this event.

FUN FACT

In 2005, Jolene Van Vugt was the first woman to backflip a full-sized dirt bike.

THE FIRST BACKFLIP

Everyone thought backflips were impossible. Motorcycles were too heavy. Carey Hart wanted to prove them wrong. He tried a backflip in 2000. He didn't land it. But he showed it was possible. Some say it didn't count.

CHAPTER 3

BIKES AND GEAR

Talia prepares for a long day of training. She is an **amateur** FMX rider. She hopes to go pro soon. There aren't many female professional FMX riders. She wants to change that.

FMX riders wear lots of safety gear. First, she puts on body armor. It's made of hard plastic. It protects her chest, ribs, and back. Some armor goes over clothes. Hers goes under. She also wears pads on her lower back, knees, and elbows. Next, she puts on her neck brace. This will spread out the pressure if she falls. It can help protect her neck during the race. Talia puts on her jersey and pants set. They are lime green. She also wears a helmet. This is the most important piece of her safety gear. Her helmet covers her whole head. She also wears goggles. They keep dirt out of her eyes.

FMX athletes wear protective gear like body armor to protect themselves in case they crash or fall.

THE BIKE

Flip lever
Steering stabilizer
Handlebars with no strut
Grab hole
Engine

Talia goes to the garage for her bike. FMX bikes are different from regular dirt bikes. FMX bikes have flip levers. These are bars above the handlebars. They help keep Talia's hands on the bike. There's no **strut** on the handlebars. This gives her room to do tricks. FMX bikes have stabilizers. They keep the handlebars straight. That's important if she's doing a **no-hander**. The bike also has grab holes. They are under the seat. She can grab them when doing tricks.

Doing tricks on a dirt bike requires lots of practice.

Some racers build their own foam pits to practice on.

FMX tracks have different sizes of ramps and landings. Talia likes doing tricks off quarterpipes. She loves the smell of the dirt in the air. But today, Talia heads to the air bag. Air bags let riders practice safely. If she falls, she has a cushion. It's like a big pillow. Some riders practice with pits of foam. But foam pits can be dangerous. Foam is flammable. The hot bike can start a fire. Riders also need a crane to get the bike out. Talia likes using the air bag. She can practice backflips.

FUN FACT
Foam pits can cost $30,000 to $50,000.

CHAPTER 4

Travis Pastrana amazed the crowd at the 2006 X Games when he performed a double backflip.

FAMOUS FREESTYLERS

The year was 2006. Travis Pastrana wanted to do something huge. He built a foam pit. He started working on a double backflip. He hadn't planned to do the trick at the X Games. He had only landed it once. The dirt landing was packed hard. Organizers told him he shouldn't do it. But he was in third place. He was inspired by the energy of the crowd. He decided to risk it all. There was a roll-in, a ramp, and the landing. Pastrana rode down the roll-in. He flew off the ramp. He flipped twice in the air. He landed perfectly! The crowd went wild. He won gold for his efforts.

FUN FACT

Travis Pastrana performs with his wife, skateboarder Lyn-z Pastrana, for Nitro Circus.

Jackson "Jacko" Strong grew up riding motorcycles. He was raised on a farm in Australia. He saved up money for his first bike by selling eggs. Soon, he started building his own ramps. Then he started doing tricks. He joined the Crusty Demons of Dirt live tour. He was just thirteen. He built a foam pit on his family farm. He practiced front flips. The X Games said it was too dangerous to do in a competition. He had to prove he could do it. He was nineteen years old when he landed the first-ever front flip in a competition. In 2018, he became the first FMX rider to win four gold medals in Best Trick.

FUN FACT

Jackson "Jacko" Strong has a rescued kangaroo named Skip.

As of 2018, Jackson "Jacko" Strong had four gold medals from the X Games.

THREE STARS OF FREESTYLE MOTOCROSS

TRAVIS PASTRANA

Travis Pastrana, an American racer, got his start in BMX racing. Then he found FMX. He has seventeen medals from seventeen X Games appearances. He was a founding member of Nitro Circus. He helped make the Nitro World Games competition a reality.

JACKSON STRONG

Jackson "Jacko" Strong is an Australian FMX rider. He was in a bad accident in 2013. His leg was hurt in an explosion. Doctors said he would never walk again. But a few months later, he ran a marathon. He returned to the X Games in 2016.

TOM PAGÈS

Tom Pagès is a French FMX rider. He is known for his bike flip. He did it for the first time at X-Fighters in Madrid, Spain. It was 2014. He won his first X Games Freestyle gold in 2018. He was the first European to win gold in FMX at the X Games. He was thirty-three years old. That made him the oldest winner.

FMX has come a long way. When it first started, no one dreamed of doing a backflip. They thought it was impossible. Now, riders do double backflips. They do front flips, too. It's exciting to think about what might come next.

Riders are often coming up with ideas for new tricks.

BEST TRICK

Many FMX competitions feature a Best Trick event. Best Trick is all about doing something new. In Freestyle, riders have to do multiple tricks in a row. In Best Trick, riders do just one trick. Travis Pastrana's double backflip was done in a Best Trick event.

BEYOND THE BOOK

After reading the book, it's time to think about what you learned. Try the following exercises to jumpstart your ideas.

THINK

THAT'S NEWS TO ME. Travis Pastrana did the first double backflip in competition at the X Games in 2006. How might news sources be able to fill in more detail about this? What new information could you find in news articles? Where could you go to find those sources?

CREATE

SHARPEN YOUR RESEARCH SKILLS. Talia wants to become a professional FMX rider someday. Where could you go in the library to find more information about female FMX riders? Who could you talk to who might know more? Create a research plan. Write a paragraph about your next steps for research.

SHARE

WHAT'S YOUR OPINION? Carey Hart did an FMX backflip in 2000. But he didn't land it. Some people say it doesn't count. Do you agree or disagree with this position? Use evidence from the text to support your answer. Share your position and evidence with a friend. Does your friend agree with you?

GROW

REAL-LIFE RESEARCH. What places could you visit to learn more about FMX riding? What other things could you learn while you were there?

RESEARCH NINJA

Visit www.ninjaresearcher.com/0653 to learn how to take your research skills and book report writing to the next level!

RESEARCH

DIGITAL LITERACY TOOLS

SEARCH LIKE A PRO

Learn about how to use search engines to find useful websites.

FACT OR FAKE?

Discover how you can tell a trusted website from an untrustworthy resource.

TEXT DETECTIVE

Explore how to zero in on the information you need most.

SHOW YOUR WORK

Research responsibly—learn how to cite sources.

WRITE

GET TO THE POINT

Learn how to express your main ideas.

PLAN OF ATTACK

Learn prewriting exercises and create an outline.

DOWNLOADABLE REPORT FORMS

FURTHER RESOURCES

BOOKS

Adamson, Thomas K. *Motocross Freestyle*. Bellwether Media, 2016.

Polydoros, Lori. *Awesome Freestyle Motocross Tricks and Stunts.* Capstone, 2011.

Ripley's Believe It or Not. *Nitro Circus: You Got This, Featuring Travis Pastrana.* Ripley Publishing, 2019.

WEBSITES

FACTSURFER

Factsurfer.com gives you a safe, fun way to find more information.

1. Go to www.factsurfer.com.
2. Enter "Freestyle Motocross" into the search box and click 🔍.
3. Select your book cover to see a list of related websites.

GLOSSARY

360: In FMX, a 360 is a trick where a rider takes off from a ramp and pulls his or her bike in a full circle. A 360 is similar to a backflip, but harder.

amateur: An amateur is someone who does something for fun, not money. Talia is an amateur competitor.

body varial: A body varial is a trick where riders leave their bikes and spin their bodies around in midair. Tom Pagès did a body varial in his gold medal run.

no-hander: A no-hander is a trick where riders take their hands off the handlebars. FMX bikes have stabilizers to keep the bike steady during a no-hander.

quarterpipe: A quarterpipe is a ramp that is shaped like half of the letter *U*. The FMX rider did a flair trick off of a quarterpipe.

roll-in: A roll-in is a big ramp to ride down and build up speed. Travis Pastrana used a roll-in to do his double backflip.

signature move: A signature move is something a rider is known for. Tom Pagès's signature move is the bike flip.

sponsors: Sponsors give money to professional riders. The early motocross sponsors had lots of strict rules, like no tattoos or long hair.

strut: A strut is a bar connecting the handlebars on a bike. FMX bikes don't have struts, so riders can do more tricks.

INDEX

PHOTO CREDITS

The images in this book are reproduced through the courtesy of: Christian Bertrand/ Shutterstock Images, front cover (biker); freelanceartist/Shutterstock Images, front cover (pattern background); OksanaNizienko/Shutterstock Images, front cover (background sky); Christian Bertrand/Shutterstock Images, pp. 3, 18; Maciej Kopaniecki/Shutterstock Images, pp. 5, 6–7; RoidRanger/Shutterstock Images, p. 8; Joerg Mitter/Red Bull/Sipa/1407011639/AP Images, pp. 8–9; sirtravelalot/Shutterstock Images, pp. 10–11; Rodrigo Garrido/Shutterstock Images, pp. 12–13, 27; Red Line Editorial, pp. 14, 26 (chart); Gerain0812/Shutterstock Images, p. 15; AlohaHawaii/Shutterstock Images, p. 16; Randy Miramontez/Shutterstock Images, p. 17; Frolova_Elena/Shutterstock Images, p. 19; Lenny Ignelzi/AP Images, pp. 20–21; Lorenzo Mondo/Shutterstock Images, pp. 21, 30; Mark J. Terrill/AP Images, p. 22; Pospisil MRL/ Shutterstock Images, p. 23; Jae C. Hong/AP Images, pp. 24–25; Peter Morgan/AP Images, p. 26 (top); Darrian Traynor/Cricket Australia/Getty Images, p. 26 (middle); Joel Saget/AFP/Getty Images, p. 26 (bottom).

ABOUT THE AUTHOR

K. A. Hale is a writer and editor from Minnesota. She enjoys reading, writing, and playing with her dog.